This
Sleepy Little Yoga book
belongs to

. . . .

To Liberty Rose with love — R. W.

For my grandson Jacob John — M. S.

Henry Holt and Company, LLC
Publishers since 1866
175 Fifth Avenue
New York, New York 10010
mackids.com

First published in the United States in 2007 by Henry Holt and Company.
Simultaneously published in the United Kingdom in 2007 by Hutchinson,
an imprint of Random House Children's Books.

Library of Congress Cataloging-in-Publication Data
Whitford, Rebecca.
Sleepy little yoga: a toddler's sleepy book of yoga / Rebecca Whitford,
Martina Selway.—1st American ed.
p. cm.
ISBN 978-0-8050-8193-0
1. Hatha yoga for children—Juvenile literature. I. Selway, Martina. II. Title.
RJ133.7W49 2007   613.7'046083—dc22   2006009248

First American Edition—2007
Printed in Malaysia by Tien Wah Press (Pte) Ltd.
9 10

Sleepy Little Yoga

Rebecca Whitford & Martina Selway

HENRY HOLT AND COMPANY
NEW YORK

hangs upside down like a

eee-eeek

bat.

Yoga Baby_

blinks her eyes like an

to-wit
to-woo

owl.

sniffs the night air like a

sniff sniff

little fox.

Yoga Baby_

flops down like a

aaaaah

tired bunny.

pushes his feet to the stars like a

stars like a

ooooooooh-ah

bear cub.

Yoga Baby–

curls up like a

snuffle

little porcupine.

hums like a

mmmmm

sleepy bee.

Yoga Baby—

floats down like a

flitter flutter

dreamy moth.

ahh, shh, shh.

A Note to Parents and Caregivers

Sleepy Little Yoga is a gentle and relaxing yoga sequence to help toddlers wind down before bedtime or a nap—whether by copying Yoga Baby and the nighttime animals, by practicing with a grown-up, or by simply reading and sharing. The poses include calming forward bends that quiet the energies and are often practiced toward the end of the day; palming the eyes, which is very restful; and bee breath, which is a soothing breathing technique. With practice, yoga can help to calm and relax toddlers by encouraging moments of quiet and stillness.

Sleepy Little Yoga is designed to be fun and relaxing, not as a manual, so allow it to take its own form and give your child lots of encouragement.

Practice Tips

• Practice with bare feet on a nonslip surface; use a clear space in a warm room and wear loose, comfortable clothing—pajamas are perfect for sleepy yoga.

• As with any form of exercise, it is best not to practice this sequence immediately after eating.

• Practice with your child so that he or she can copy you.

• Use your own judgment about your child's ability and let your child move at his or her own pace, giving support when necessary.

• Encourage your child to try poses but do not look for or expect perfection. Above all, *Sleepy Little Yoga* is meant to be an enjoyable, positive experience.

• Don't force your toddler into a pose or let him or her hold any pose for too long.

• Allow your child to play with a pose before moving on to the next one.

• Encourage your child to keep his or her breath flowing—toddlers are too young to practice controlled breathing—and to move slowly in and out of poses.

• Simple stories can help your Yoga Baby relax when in the resting pose.

• The photos that follow are not precise because they are a real reflection of how our toddlers have interpreted the poses.

Most important, keep your *Sleepy Little Yoga* practice **simple** and **playful!**

Explanation of Poses

Bat (Standing Forward Bend)—from a wide-legged standing position raise arms up. Fold forward from the hips, letting head, hands, and the upper body relax down to the floor. Keep knees bent if more comfortable. Slowly uncurl to a standing position.

Owl (Palming the Eyes)—sit back on heels with a straight spine and eyes wide open. Close and open the eyes two or three times. Rub palms together in front of the chest to create warmth, then lower the head and gently place the palms over closed eyes. Stay until the warmth fades, then repeat.

Fox (Kneeling Upward Stretch)—from sitting on heels, move up onto knees while sweeping arms above the head. Then stretch up with palms facing each other. Lift the chin and look up.

Bunny (Kneeling Forward Bend)—from fox pose with arms outstretched, sink hips/bottom onto heels, bend forward, and lower chest to thighs and forehead to the floor. Hold and relax.

Bear Cub (Upward Raised Legs)—from a lying position, knees drawn in over the chest and arms alongside the body with palms down, straighten legs and raise heels toward the ceiling and try to keep chin tucked in. Bend the knees in and repeat.

Porcupine (Knees to Chest)—from bear cub pose, hug knees to chest, then move the head and upper body toward the knees, trying to keep chin tucked in. Relax head and torso down to the floor.

Bee (Bee Breath)—in a sitting position bend the knees, bring the soles of the feet together, and keep spine straight. Rest the hands on the knees, close the eyes, and breathe in through the nose. Keeping the lips gently closed, breathe out with a slow, steady hum—*mmmm*. Repeat breathing several times.

Moth—from a sitting position with bent knees and the soles of the feet together, hold the toes, sit with a straight spine, bend the elbows, and fold forward, relaxing the head toward the feet. Relax knees out to the side. Sit up slowly and gently bring knees together.

Rest (Savasana)—lie on back, keeping body in a straight line. With legs hip-width apart, let feet relax out to the sides. Keep arms slightly away from the body and the palms faced down. Try to keep head in line with the spine. Close the eyes and imagine drifting on a cloud through the night, past the moon and the stars. . . .

Bat (Standing Forward Bend)

Owl (Palming the Eyes)

Bunny (Kneeling Forward Bend)

Fox (Kneeling Upward Stretch)

Bear Cub (Upward Raised Legs)

Porcupine (Knees to chest)

Bee (Bee Breath)

Moth

Rest (Savasana)